THE SOVIET UNION
A PORTRAIT

Read for accuracy by

Series Consultant
David McDonald
Professor of History
University of Wisconsin—Madison

Library of Congress Number: 89-3687

1 2 3 4 5 6 7 8 9   94 93 92 91 90 89

Library of Congress Cataloging-in-Publication Data

Clark, James I.
  The Soviet Union : a portrait / James I. Clark.
  (Portrait of the Soviet Union)
  Includes index.
  Summary: Focuses on the history, geography, ethnic groups, arts, government, and people of the Soviet Union.
  1. Soviet Union—Juvenile literature. [1. Soviet Union.] I. Title.
II. Series: Clark, James I. Portrait of the Soviet Union.
DK266.C565   1989   947—dc19   89-3687
ISBN 0-8172-3351-2 (hardcover)
ISBN 0-8172-3361-X (softcover)

Cover Photo: TBS/Reagan

THE SOVIET UNION
A PORTRAIT

James I. Clark

RAINTREE PUBLISHERS
Milwaukee

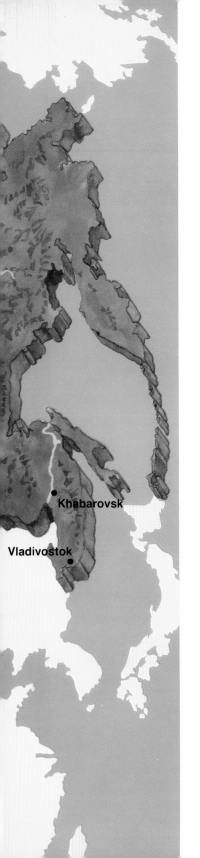

Khabarovsk

Vladivostok

CONTENTS

INTRODUCTION

The land now known as the Union of Soviet Socialist Republics was once called Russia. Russia's beginning as a nation dates to the middle of the ninth century A.D., when Slavic people of Novgorod asked Vikings called Varangian Russes to bring order to their land. The Viking Rurik was Russia's first ruler. Later, Kiev became the center of government, and for a time the land was known as Kievan Russia.

Christianity came to Russia in 988 under Vladimir I. He chose the Eastern Orthodox faith for himself and his people, making the Russian Orthodox Church the official church. At about the same time, the Cyrillic alphabet was adopted and Russian became a written language.

War frequently visited the land, and in the 1200s Russia came under the control of Mongols, a people from the east. Mongol rule, chiefly through Russian officials who collected taxes for the invaders, was to last for more than two hundred years.

Mongol control reached its twilight stage under the Russian ruler Ivan III, a descendant of Rurik, in the late 1400s. During the time of Ivan III, Russia gained land to the west, and Moscow became the most important city. Ivan III called himself czar, or emperor. His grandson Ivan IV was the first to be crowned czar, in 1547.

By the time of Catherine the Great, Russia's borders were extended to the Black Sea.

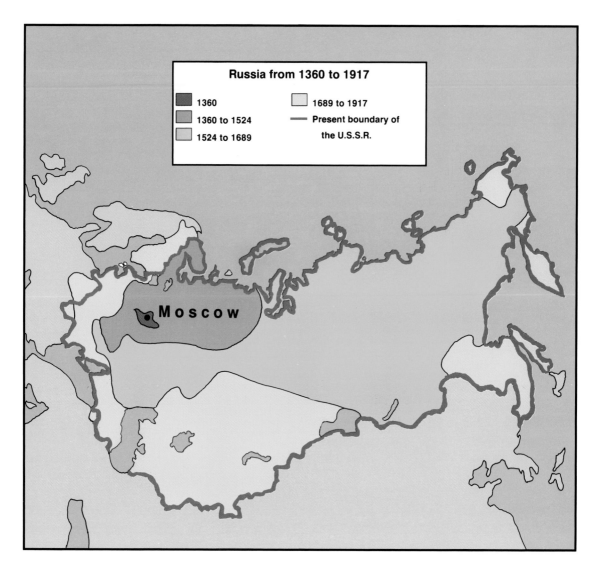

Russia from 1360 to 1917

- 1360
- 1360 to 1524
- 1524 to 1689
- 1689 to 1917
- Present boundary of the U.S.S.R.

MOSCOW

Russia Under the Czars

Under Ivan IV, called "the Terrible" because of his cruelty, the Russian nation expanded into Siberia. Ivan IV made Moscow the nation's capital, and he also began the system of serfdom in Russia. Peasants whom the czar made serfs could no longer leave the land on which they had been born. If land was sold, serfs were sold with it. Over the centuries, by order of one czar or another, the number of serfs in Russia grew into the millions.

The time after the death of Ivan

IV in 1584 was one of turmoil and confusion. There were wars with Poland and Lithuania and civil war within the nation. Order finally came in 1613, when nobles and landowners chose Michael Romanov as czar. The Romanovs would rule Russia for 304 years.

Two Romanovs of the 1700s became known as "the Great." They were Peter I and Catherine II.

Peter I sought to bring Western ways and ideas to Russia, and he traveled in several European countries to learn firsthand what life was like there. Peter also had a new city built on the Baltic Sea. Naming it St. Petersburg, he made the new city Russia's capital. It would be the nation's "window to the West."

Catherine II, a German princess, married Grand Duke Peter, also a German, who was later crowned as Czar Peter III. She became Russia's sole ruler after she helped Peter's enemies remove him from the throne. Peter was later murdered. Catherine II expanded Russian territory into Poland and along the Black Sea. She also greatly increased the number of serfs in Russia.

Paul, son of Catherine II, fol-

Top of page: *a small visitor admires the fountains of Peter the Great's Leningrad palace, the Petrovorets. Above: a bedroom furnished in the baroque style favored by Catherine the Great.*

lowed her to the throne. He was murdered five years later and his son became czar as Alexander I.

Russia had no constitution and no representative government. The people had only the rights the czar saw fit to grant them, and those were few. Since the time of Ivan IV, a watchful secret police had imprisoned anyone who criticized the government. Alexander I freed many of those prisoners. He made it easier for Russians to travel to other countries. He abolished torture as a means for police to gain confessions from those accused of crimes. And he had a constitution written, although it never went into effect. Alexander also brought glory to Russia as an invading French army of 600,000 under Napoleon I met disastrous defeat in 1812.

Desire for a constitution and rule by law instead of by czars and nobles only grew among young army officers and among some of the nobility as well. Thousands of them gathered in St. Petersburg in December 1825 to voice their de-

A drawing shows the attempted shooting of Alexander II during a state visit to French emperor Napoleon III in 1867. An assassin's bomb finally killed the czar in 1881.

Nicholas II dealt harshly with dissenters.

mands to the new czar, Nicholas I. He ordered troops to fire on them and later had leaders of the Decembrist Revolt hanged. Government control now became tighter.

Alexander II succeeded Nicholas I, and he is best remembered as the czar who freed the serfs in 1861. He also granted towns and villages some self-government and allowed his people the right of trial by jury.

The desire for greater change remained alive in Russia, however. Members of a revolutionary group called "The People's Will" concluded that only the death of the czar would bring lasting change. They tried several times to assassinate Alexander II and finally succeeded in 1881.

This had a severe reverse effect. Upon becoming czar, Alexander III abolished most of the changes Alexander II had made, except freedom for the serfs.

Nicholas II, crowned czar in 1894, was a handsome, kind, and gentle man. He had little interest in the duties of government, however, and he proved to be the wrong man to rule Russia during the new time of troubles that were ahead.

Problems began in 1904, with the birth of a son, Alexis, who had hemophilia. This later brought the czarina, Alexandra, under the influence of a holy man nicknamed Rasputin, who showed that he could control Alexis's bleeding and could cure the boy's headaches. As a result of his value to Alexis, Rasputin's influence also grew in matters of government, which caused nobles to fear and hate him.

The elected Duma was created following civil uprisings in 1905. In the scene above, workers raise barricades in the streets of St. Petersburg.

The Revolution

In 1904-1905, Russia fought and lost a brief war with Japan. Early in 1905, troops fired on a crowd of thousands who came to the Winter Palace in St. Petersburg to ask the czar for a constitution and representative government. Defeat in battle and bloodshed at home brought the fury of the people down on Nicholas II. Revolution seemed near.

Nicholas II finally granted representative government in the form of an elected Duma, which was a legislative body but had limited powers. He kept supreme authority to himself, however. Then in 1914, Russia once again was at war, fighting along with France and England against Germany and Austria-Hungary.

World War I cost Russia the lives of millions of soldiers, defeats in the hands of German armies, and much hardship at home. People's anger with the czar grew more intense, and mobs of hungry people rioted. Sent to put down the riots, the czar's soldiers joined the mobs instead. Finally, Nicholas II abdicated, giving up his right to the throne. Russia would have no more czars.

AFTER THE REVOLUTION

A new government took over in Russia as Nicholas II gave up the throne following the first revolution in 1917. That government was controlled by several groups. One important group believed that change should come to Russia in a democratic way and that Russia should continue in the war against Germany.

In the meantime, another group of revolutionaries, called Bolsheviks, sought power in Russia. The Bolsheviks were led by Vladimir Ilyich Ulyanov, better known by his revolutionary name, Lenin.

Lenin was born in 1870 in a small village on the Volga River. He studied law at a university, but his real interest was in revolution. Lenin's aim became to establish Communist rule in Russia.

His devotion to revolution got Lenin in trouble with the police. He was sent to Siberia for three years and was then allowed to leave Russia. Lenin lived in Germany, England, Sweden, and Switzerland at various times. He was in Switzerland when the czar was

overthrown. Lenin quickly returned to Russia, hoping to lead the Bolsheviks to power there.

Russian peasants wanted land. People in cities wanted food. Nearly everyone wanted Russia out of the war. The government, however, did not meet any of those demands.

Lenin and his followers tried to seize control of the government. They failed, and Lenin fled to Finland. He returned to Russia in 1917 and again urged his followers to take over. This time, the Bolsheviks succeeded with a second

Russia was brought under communist control after Lenin urged his followers to overthrow the weak government which replaced the czar.

Under communism, land was reorganized into large collective farms. Above is a beet field on a modern collective in the Ukraine.

revolution as the weak government disappeared overnight. Now in control, the Bolsheviks changed their name to the Russian Communist party.

Among the first acts of the Communist government was to make a peace treaty with Germany. Peace did not come to Russia, however, until after a bloody civil war between Red Communist forces and White anti-Communist armies that sought to overthrow the new government.

Not until 1921 was the Communist government secure in Russia. Moscow became the nation's capital once again. Petrograd became Leningrad, and Russia became the Union of Soviet Socialist Republics.

Under Lenin's leadership, the government took over land, factories, banks, and railroads. This did not work out well. The nation's production of food and factory goods decreased. The government then backed off. It returned small factories to private ownership and gave land to peasant families.

Lenin died in 1924. Josif Vissarionovich Djugashvili, better known as Joseph Stalin, won the struggle for control of the Communist party and the government. Stalin, who was in conflict with moderate people in government, now began to make changes. Once again, the government took over all land and factories. In 1929, land was turned into collective farms, which the government controlled. The peasants who worked on the farms were paid mainly with a share of the crop. The number of state farms, where peasants were paid wages, was increased. Peasants fought hard against the idea of collectives, and several million peasants were killed or sent to prison in Siberia as a result.

Stalin ruled as a dictator. There was no freedom of thought, movement, speech, or the press. Secret police kept tabs on everyone. Although they lacked many freedoms, citizens of the Soviet Union were guaranteed jobs, a place to live, an education, and medical care.

Under Stalin, the Soviet Union became a strong industrial nation, producing iron and steel, locomotives, machinery, electrical power, and oil and natural gas. By the eve

After the revolution, Moscow (below) was made capital of the new Soviet state.

of World War II, it also had become a strong military power.

World War II began in 1939, with Germany on one side and England, France, and Poland on the other. The Soviet Union remained friendly toward Germany. When Germany defeated Poland, the two nations split that country between them. The Soviet Union also gained control of the Baltic states. After Germany conquered much of Europe, England fought on alone. Then in June 1941, Germany invaded the Soviet Union. In December of that year the United States entered the war, to fight alongside England and the Soviet Union against Germany.

The Soviet Union suffered great losses in World War II. At least twenty million soldiers and civilians died. Thousands of villages, towns, and cities were destroyed. Yet Soviet armies pushed the Germans back as English and American armies invaded Europe in the West. The war ended with German defeat in 1945.

After the war, the Soviet Union

World War II has remained as a living memory for the Soviet people. At left are memorials to the war dead in Leningrad cemetaries.

established Communist governments in Poland, Hungary, Rumania, Bulgaria, Czechoslovakia, Yugoslavia, Albania, and East Germany. The Soviet government insisted that it simply wanted friendly governments on its western border to protect it against invasion in years to come. However, believing that the Soviet Union really aimed to take over all of Europe, nations of Western Europe and the United States responded by building up armed forces. A period of great distrust between other nations and the Soviet Union began, a period called the Cold War.

Relations between the Soviet Union and the United States improved somewhat after Stalin died in 1953, during the leadership of Nikita Khrushchev. Soviet society became somewhat more open, too. Scientists and artists were allowed greater freedom, the workweek was cut to forty hours, and workers were allowed to change jobs if they wished. At the same time, factory and farm production increased, and the Soviet people enjoyed better lives than they had under Stalin.

There were some times of tension, however. The Soviet Union

brought down an American spy plane in its territory in 1960, and in 1962 Americans discovered that the U.S.S.R. had built missile bases in Cuba, a Communist nation about ninety miles south of Florida's coast. The Soviet Union called off a planned conference between Khrushchev and President Dwight D. Eisenhower after the spy plane incident. The Soviet Union and the United States moved to the brink of war over the missiles in Cuba before the Soviets removed them.

Under the leadership of Leonid Brezhnev, relations with the United States remained fairly good during the 1960s and 1970s. In the late 1970s they soured, however, over the issue of the lack of human rights in the Soviet Union and that nation's invasion of Afghanistan to prop up a weak Communist government there.

By the time Brezhnev died in 1982, farm and factory production had slowed considerably. The economy was almost standing still, and there was great discontent among workers and the population in general. In addition, the greater freedom Soviet citizens had enjoyed following Stalin's death had nearly disappeared.

Mikhail Gorbachev became

In 1987 General Secretary Gorbachev and President Reagan signed a treaty limiting Soviet and American arsenals of nuclear weapons.

Above: *American wheat is loaded on a Soviet grain boat. The Soviet Union's inability to produce enough grain for its own needs has made the country an important market for U.S. agricultural exports.*

head of the Communist party and the government in 1985. Gorbachev promised great change in the Soviet Union. He spoke of g*losnost,* which means "openness," and of *perestroika,* which means "restructuring" or "making over." *Glosnost* would mean greater freedom for citizens, even to the point that they could safely criticize the government. *Perestroika* would mean change in the economic system, the way manufactured goods, services, and food are produced and distributed. There would be less government involvement, and more private farm and business activity.

Gorbachev met five times with President Ronald Reagan. The Soviet Union and the United States agreed to reduce the number of nuclear weapons each nation had. The Soviet Union withdrew from Afghanistan in 1989. Also, it cut its armed forces by 500,000. It also planned to reduce the amount of money it spent on the military.

Mikhail Gorbachev spoke of changes he wanted to make as a "revolution." Certainly they would be greater changes than the people of the Soviet Union had known for many years.

LAND AND OTHER RESOURCES

More than 6,000 miles (9,656 kilometers) separate the Soviet Union's eastern and western borders. The longest distance north to south is 3,200 miles (5,150 km). Altogether, the U.S.S.R. covers 8,649,500 square miles (22,402,000 sq. km). It has 30,787 miles (49,547 km) of coastline.

Much of the land is made up of plains. The old and worn Carpathian Mountains form part of the southwestern border of the European Plain. The high Caucasus Mountains lie to the south, between the Black and Caspian seas. The gently rolling land of the European Plain runs east to the Ural Mountains. Many streams and rivers crisscross it, including the Volga, the Dniester, the Dnieper, the Don, and the Western and Northern Dvinia.

A land region by themselves, the Ural Mountains were formed 225 million years ago. Today, they are little more than rounded hills of from 1,000 to 6,000 feet (300 to 1,800 meters) in elevation.

The West Siberia Plain is the largest plains region in the world, covering more than 1 million square miles (2.6 million sq. km). The most important rivers of this region are the Ob and the Irtysh. They rise in the Alta Mountains along the Chinese-Mongolian border, and flow northward into the Kara Sea, part of the Arctic Ocean. During much of the year, the northern reaches of the Ob-Irtysh waterway are frozen.

To the east of the West Siberian Plain is the Central Siberian Plateau. The region extends east to the Verkhoyansk Mountains and south to the Sayan and Baikal mountains. Hundreds of rivers and streams cut through the region, and its outstanding body of water is Lake Baikal, the largest and deepest freshwater lake in the world.

The East Siberian Uplands make up the Soviet Union's largest region. Most of it is mountainous, with peaks rising as high as 10,000 feet (3,050 m).

Soviet Central Asia lies to the south of the West Siberian Plain. The region stretches from the Caspian Sea to the Chinese border. Much of it is at or below sea level, and it is a region of great deserts.

A river cuts through the rugged Caucasus.

Temperature and Humidity
For Selected Cities

VLADIVOSTOK

	Degrees Fahrenheit		Degrees Celsius		Humidity
	High	Low	High	Low	Percent
JAN.	13	0	-11	-18	65
FEB.	22	6	- 6	-14	64
MAR.	33	19	1	- 7	66
APR.	46	34	8	1	70
MAY	55	43	13	6	74
JUNE	63	52	17	11	83
JULY	71	60	22	16	85
AUG.	75	64	24	18	82
SEPT.	68	55	20	13	75
OCT.	55	41	13	5	65
NOV.	36	24	2	- 4	63
DEC.	20	8	- 7	-13	64

IRKUTSK

	Degrees Fahrenheit		Degrees Celsius		Humidity
	High	Low	High	Low	Percent
JAN.	3	-15	-16	-26	80
FEB.	10	-13	-12	-25	74
MAR.	25	2	- 4	-17	69
APR.	42	20	6	- 7	59
MAY	56	33	13	1	54
JUNE	68	44	20	7	60
JULY	70	50	21	10	70
AUG.	68	48	20	9	73
SEPT.	57	35	14	2	72
OCT.	41	21	5	- 6	72
NOV.	20	2	- 7	-17	80
DEC.	4	-12	-16	-24	87

Mountains border Soviet Central Asia on the south.

Generally speaking, the Soviet Union has a continental climate, featuring long, cold winters and short, warm summers. There are differences within the overall climate, however. These range from a polar climate in the north to a desert climate in certain areas in the south. Temperatures lower than -90° Fahrenheit (-68° Celsius) have been recorded in northern Siberia. Summer temperatures in southern desert regions have run as high as 120°F (49°C).

Precipitation averages more than 30 inches (75 centimeters) on the European Plain and in parts of the East Siberian Uplands. Much of the country, though, receives from 5 to 10 inches (12.7 to 25.4 cm) of precipitation a year.

Land regions of the Soviet Union include the tundra, the taiga, the steppe, and the desert. A fifth and tiny zone is subtropical.

The tundra is a treeless plain running along the Arctic Ocean. Temperatures on the tundra average far below freezing for nine months of the year.

Taiga means "forest" in Russian, and this is a band of continuous forest that runs for 5,000 miles (8,000 km) east and west and from 600 to 1,200 miles (965 to 1,930 km) north and south. Winters are long and cold in the taiga, but summers are warm. Larch, pine, spruce, and fir are the principal trees. Such hardwoods as maple and oak are found in the western part of the region.

In the south, the taiga gives way to the steppe, a grasslands region. This level region runs for 1,000 miles (1,600 km) from Kazakhstan in Central Asia west to the Ukrainian and Moldavian republics. The eastern part of the steppe is an ideal grazing area. The western part is outstanding for farming.

The main deserts of Central Asia are the Kara Kum, or "black sands," and the Kyzyl Kum, or "red sands." The desert soil is fertile, and it can be farmed with proper irrigation.

A subtropical, or Mediterranean, region is located along the western shore of the Black Sea. Another such area is found in the southern part of the Crimean Peninsula, which thrusts into the Black Sea.

The Soviet Union is rich in natural resources. About 5.5 million acres (2.2 million hectares) of land

Temperature and Humidity For Selected Cities

KIEV					
	Degrees Fahrenheit		Degrees Celsius		Humidity
	High	Low	High	Low	Percent
JAN.	24	14	- 4	-10	84
FEB.	28	17	- 2	- 8	81
MAR.	37	25	3	- 4	78
APR.	56	41	14	5	67
MAY	69	51	21	11	60
JUNE	75	56	24	14	61
JULY	77	59	25	15	63
AUG.	76	58	24	14	67
SEPT.	68	50	20	10	67
OCT.	56	42	13	6	76
NOV.	42	32	6	0	87
DEC.	30	22	- 1	- 6	87

MOSCOW					
	Degrees Fahrenheit		Degrees Celsius		Humidity
	High	Low	High	Low	Percent
JAN.	15	3	- 9	-16	80
FEB.	22	8	- 6	-14	74
MAR.	32	18	0	- 8	73
APR.	50	34	10	1	64
MAY	66	46	19	8	51
JUNE	70	51	21	11	55
JULY	73	55	23	13	61
AUG.	72	53	22	12	65
SEPT.	61	45	16	7	69
OCT.	48	37	9	3	74
NOV.	35	26	2	- 3	83
DEC.	24	15	- 5	-10	84

Chart Design: Eileen Rickey

Inside the cow shed at a Ukrainian state farm. Large farms like this keep dairy herds of about six hundred animals.

can be farmed. In addition, the nation leads the world in the production of iron ore, coal, oil, natural gas, diamonds, and gold. Its huge forests make it a leading producer of wood and wood products. Many rivers have been dammed to store water for irrigation and to produce electric power.

Important resources, such as oil, gas, and copper, have been discovered in the far north. Ways have been found for humans to live fairly comfortably through the long, cold winters while extracting and transporting mineral resources from the region.

There is some farming in cleared areas of the taiga and wheat, rye, and oats are grown on short-grass steppe land east of the Urals. There, however, rainfall amounts to about 20 inches (50 cm) a year, and it is unreliable. The eastern steppe region is best suited for grazing.

The heartland of farming in the Soviet Union lies to the west of the Urals. Located there are great fields of wheat, corn, rye, barley, and sugar beets. Dairy farming is an important occupation, too, and cattle are also raised for their meat. Fruits and vegetables are the most important crops on farms on the small areas of Mediterranean climate in the southwest.

Thousands of farms are organized as state farms. These farms often concentrate on one crop, such as potatoes or corn. Workers on state farms are paid wages, just like factory workers. Thousands of other farms are organized as collective farms. Here farmers are paid with a share of the crop and with money, after crops are sold and expenses are paid. Farm families may have small plots of land for their own use. They may sell crops they raise on such land and keep the income.

Older manufacturing centers in the Soviet Union are located in

In Siberia, sturgeon from Lake Baikal are harvested for their yield of eggs . . . the famous Russian caviar.

Galen Rowell/Mountain Light

Distribution of Important Food Products in the U.S.S.R.

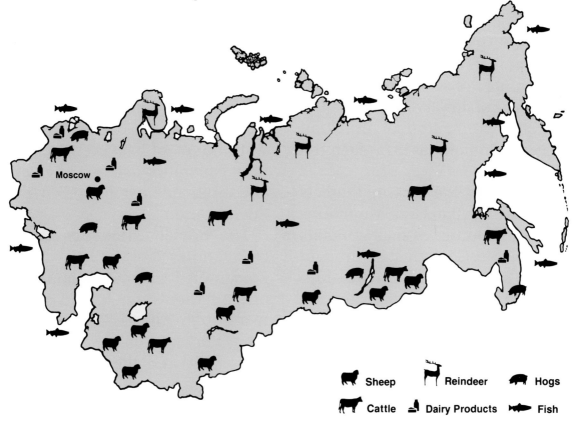

Moscow

Sheep Reindeer Hogs

Cattle Dairy Products Fish

The U.S.S.R. is the world's largest single producer of coal, responsible for one-quarter of annual world production. Coal is the country's most important fuel for generating electric power.

and around such cities as Moscow and Leningrad. Factories in those cities produce electrical equipment, cars, chemicals, and machinery of all kinds. The Donets Basis of the Ukraine is a center for the production of iron and steel and numerous manufactured products.

Although the wealth there is decreasing, the Ural Mountains are still a source of such minerals as iron ore. Coal must be brought to the region, but within the Urals, Magitogorsk has long been an important iron and steel center. Oil fields are also found in the Urals.

The Caspian Sea and the land around it are also sources of oil for the Soviet Union. Other large oil fields are found in the Ukraine and around Lake Baikal in the east.

Coal and oil are the main sources of power to generate electricity. At the same time, billions of kilowatt hours of electricity come from generators at dams on rivers and from nuclear plants in the Soviet Union.

The Soviet Union has about 89,000 miles (144,000 km) of railroad track. Trains carry about half of the nation's freight and about two-thirds of the passenger traffic. Lines fan out from Moscow in all directions, and the longest line runs from Moscow to Vladivostok, on the Pacific Ocean, a total of 5,600 miles (9,000 km). Another railroad parallels the Trans-Siberian from west of Lake Baikal to the Pacific. This is BAM, the Baikal-Amur Mainline.

Long-distance auto travel in the Soviet Union is difficult because of the lack of good, all-weather roads. This is especially true in Siberia, where the land is frozen during much of the year and turns to mud and bog during the spring thaw. Altogether, the Soviet Union has about 480,000 miles (772,485 km) of highways, roads, and streets and about twelve million automobiles.

Waterways and canals in the Soviet Union are used as freight routes. There is one airline—Aeroflot—which is owned by the government.

More than sixty rivers and canals wind through Leningrad. The city is sometimes called "the Venice of the North."

half. Ukrainians are the next largest group, followed by Belorussians. Large groups of Turkic people are found in Soviet Central Asia, among them Uzbeks, Kazakhs, Kirghiz, and Turkmen. Azerbaijanis, Armenians, and Georgians occupy the southwestern part of the Soviet Union. Population growth has been greatest among non-Russian peoples, especially those of Soviet Central Asia. About two-thirds of all the Soviet people live in cities, and the movement from rural to urban areas continues.

REPUBLICS OF THE SOVIET UNION

The Soviet Union is divided into fifteen republics, according to majority ethnic groups. In addition, it is further divided into thirty-eight special regions, many of them called autonomous republics. These are organized on the basis of minority ethnic groups. For example, the Russian Soviet Federated Socialist Republic is made up mostly of Russians. Within it is the Yakut Autonomous Republic, consisting mainly of Yakuts, a Turkic people.

By far the largest part of the Soviet Union, the Russian Soviet Federated Socialist Republic takes

TBS/Reagan

Muslims observe Friday afternoon prayers in Tashkent, Uzbekistan.

Slavic ethnic groups make up the majority of the Soviet Union's population. Russians alone account for slightly more than one-

MAP OF THE SOVIET REPUBLICS

Lithuania
Estonia
Russian S.F.S.R
Latvia
Belorussia
Moldavia
Ukraine
Russian S.F.S.R
Georgia
Armenia
Kazakhstan
Azerbaijan
Turkmenistan
Uzbekistan
Kirghizia
Tadzhikistan

up three-fourths of the entire nation. It includes what is often called European Russia and Siberia as well, and holds about 143 million people.

The western part of the Russian Republic is an area of fertile farmland and large cities. Moscow, the nation's capital, is the largest city, with more than eight million people. The Kremlin, at one time a fortress, is the center for the Soviet government and the Communist party. Leningrad, formerly St. Pet-

The center of Soviet government is the Kremlin.

The city of Nizhny Novgorod was re-named Gorky to honor Soviet writer Maxim Gorky (right), shown here with Stalin in 1931.

gold, diamonds, tin, and coal. The region also has large deposits of oil and natural gas. It also has many dams where generators produce hydroelectric power. Factories in Siberia turn out iron and steel, farm machinery, building materials, and chemicals. Farms produce wheat, barley, rye, and other crops. Novoskibirsk, or "New Siberia," is the region's most important city.

The Yakuts make up one non-Russian minority group within the R.S.F.S.R. They are a hardy people, well adapted to frigid winters. Many of them worked to build a branch line of the Baikal-Amur Mainline to the city of Yakutsk.

Other Soviet republics form an arc that borders the R.S.F.S.R. from the northwest to the south and then east into Central Asia. Estonia, Latvia, and Lithuania are republics on the Baltic Sea. During the 1920s and 1930s, those republics were independent nations. The Soviet Union took them over during World War II. The chief cities and manufacturing centers of the Baltic republics are their capitals—Tallinn in Estonia, Riga in Latvia, and Vilnius in Lithuania.

The small Belorussian Republic

ersburg northwest of Moscow, has about four million people. Gorky, located east of Moscow, is a center of automobile manufacturing. It was once known as Nizhny Novgorod. It was later renamed after the famous writer Maxim Gorky.

Russian rule over Siberia dates to the 1500s, when fur traders first moved into that vast region of long, cold winters and great resources. Mines in Siberia produce lies south of the Baltic republics. Minsk, a city of about 1.5 million people, is the republic's capital and major city.

Kiev, called "the mother" of Russia, is the capital of the Ukrainian Republic, located south of Belorussia. The Russian nation began in Kiev in the 800s, and today the city is a bustling trade and manufacturing center. The republic has a population of about fifty million.

The Moldavia Republic is the second smallest. It once was known as Bessarabia, and it became part of Russia in the 1800s. Moldavia is famous for its wines, and farmers there raise numerous fruits besides grapes. They also raise sunflowers, soybeans, dairy cattle, and hogs. Kishinev is the republic's main city and capital.

Georgia, Armenia, and Azerbaijan are called the Transcaucasus Republics. They lie south of the Caucasus Mountains. Georgia is a

The production of ferrous metals has been a Soviet industrial priority since the time of Stalin. Iron and steel works are centered around the city of Kiev.

TBS/Reagan

Tblisi (above) is the capital of Georgia. Czar Paul I annexed Georgia in 1801.

land of mountains and narrow valleys, with the Black Sea bordering it on the west. It was once an independent nation ruled by kings. Russia took over Georgia early in the 1800s. The republic's capital is Tbilisi, a city of 1.5 million people.

Armenia, or the Armenian Republic, is located southwest of Georgia and west of Azerbaijan. It is the smallest republic in the Soviet Union. Armenians trace their nation back to more than a thousand years before Christ, and

for many centuries it was independent. The land fell under Turkish rule in the 1400s. During the 1920s it was divided between Turkey and the Soviet Union.

In Georgia and Armenia, the religious background is Christian. In Azerbaijan, the faith of Islam is the main religion. Today, the republic has about 6.7 million people. Oil production and refining are major industries. Azerbaijan is also known for its production of cotton, wheat, rice, fruit, and silkworms.

The five Central Asian republics occupy land from the Caspian Sea east to the Chinese border and south to the borders of Afghanistan and Iran. Most of the people are of Turkic background, and most belong to the Islamic faith. The history of the area is one of caravans carrying trade goods and of endless wars and conquests.

Turkmenistan, the Turkmen Republic, lies east of the Caspian Sea, south of the R.S.F.S.R., west of the Uzbek Republic, and north of Iran and Afghanistan. Two-thirds of the three million or so people are Turkmen, and life in the Turkmen Republic is a mixture of ancient and modern. People live in vurtas—traditional tents made of wood, rush mats, and felt—and in modern apartment buildings. Both vurtas and apartments have telephones and the latest in modern appliances. The Kara Kum desert is located in Turkmenia, and irrigated fields produce cotton, grain, and fruits and vegetables.

In Uzbekistan, the Uzbek Republic, the sun shines 250 days of the year. About half of the republic is desert, but farmers produce two-thirds of the Soviet Union's cotton with irrigation. Tashkent, the capital, is a center for the manufacture of cotton-picking machinery and cotton textiles.

Tadzhikistan is a mountainous land. Year-round glaciers fill high valleys of the Pamir Mountains. Summers are hot and dry, and winters are cold. The republic's capital, Dushambe, is a city of

Children play in the streets of Khiva, in the Uzbek Republic.

Andrew Stawicki

about a half-million people. Factories there process food and produce cotton textiles.

The Kirghiz Republic, Kirghizia, is also a mountainous land. The Tien Shan mountain range runs along its southern border with China. It is also a land of horses—250,000 of them at last count—and a land of sheep. Farmers produce sugar beets, cotton, wheat, and barley under irrigation. The republic also produces coal, lead, mercury, antimony, and uranium.

Kazakhstan, the Kazakh Republic, is the second largest in the Soviet Union after the R.S.F.S.R., which borders Kazakhstan on the north. The republic is made up mostly of plains and hilly lowlands, and the climate is dry. Irrigation is necessary to produce cotton, rice, and sugar beets, and the republic has large deposits of coal, copper, lead, oil, and natural gas. The city of Leninsk, on the Syr Darya River, is the Soviet Union's nuclear testing and space center.

Below each pair of Russian letters is its Roman equivalent (in blue).

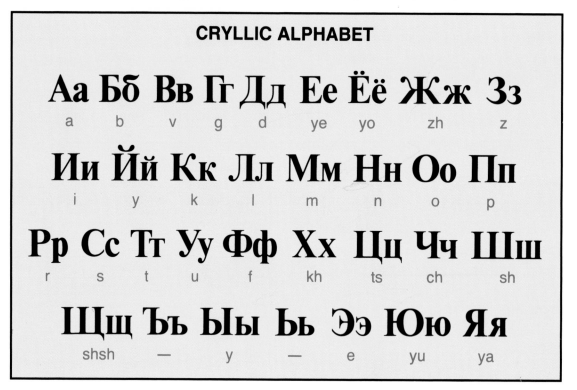

CRYLLIC ALPHABET

Аа	Бб	Вв	Гг	Дд	Ее	Ёё	Жж	Зз
a	b	v	g	d	ye	yo	zh	z

Ии	Йй	Кк	Лл	Мм	Нн	Оо	Пп
i	y	k	l	m	n	o	p

Рр	Сс	Тт	Уу	Фф	Хх	Цц	Чч	Шш
r	s	t	u	f	kh	ts	ch	sh

Щщ	Ъъ	Ыы	Ьь	Ээ	Юю	Яя
shsh	—	y	—	e	yu	ya

WAY OF LIFE

A people's culture refers to their entire way of life. It includes language, beliefs, customs, traditions, ways of rearing and educating children, and forms of popular entertainment, as well as how people express themselves in art, music, and literature.

The Soviet Union contains 170 different ethnic groups or nationalities, and thus, many cultures. Slightly more than half the people are Russian, and Russian is the major language and the major culture.

Since its beginning, the government of the Soviet Union has sought to "Russify" the nation. It has placed Russians in non-Russian republics and has required that Russian be taught in all schools. Still, differences among ethnic groups remain, especially in rural areas.

Besides Russian, there are 129 other languages and dialects spoken in the Soviet Union. Russian and most other languages are written in the Cyrillic alphabet, and there are four others in use. They are the Armenian, Georgian, Latin (or Roman), and Hebrew alphabets.

Soviet law requires that a cou-

An official state ceremony marries this couple at the Wedding Palace in Tblisi.

ple be married in a civil ceremony. That is, the ceremony must be performed by a government official. A couple may also have a religious ceremony if they wish. Most civil ceremonies are held in "marriage palaces."

A newly married couple in a city will likely begin life together in a one-room apartment of about 100 square feet (9 sq. m), with a small bathroom and kitchen. A person who wants a larger apartment will have to go on a waiting list or find someone who will trade larger for smaller.

Small living space and the fact

35

Above: *a nursery school at a collective farm near Moscow. Day-care and schooling are provided for the children of workers.*

that many women work outside the home help explain the great number of one-child families in the Soviet Union. Women make up about one-half the labor force. About four-fifths of all women have jobs outside the home in unskilled, skilled, and professional occupations.

There are about a hundred thousand nurseries or day-care centers in the Soviet Union, but this does not fill the need for working mothers. Private babysitters are hard to find. Grandparents might help out, but there are fewer of them nearby in cities than in rural areas.

For the most part, caring for children at home, grocery shopping, preparing meals, and doing laundry and cleaning remain tasks for working as well as nonworking mothers. Many women complain that husbands do not help enough or not at all.

A child in the Soviet Union enters kindergarten at age four. Studies begin in earnest at age six, upon starting grade one of a primary school. In primary school, pupils study Russian and another language, arithmetic, history, and geography. They also become acquainted with simple mathematics, chemistry, physics, and biology. Homework gradually increases to two or three hours per night.

The "incomplete" secondary program takes in grades five through nine. After that, a student might attend a special school to learn a technical skill. Or the student might remain in school for the "complete" secondary program to prepare for further schooling in a profession.

Most learning at all levels of schooling is by memorization. Students are graded on their performance with a 5 for highest and a 1 for lowest.

In their classes, students also

learn about the three Ps—politics, the party, and patriotism. They develop loyalty to their country and to the Communist party through reading, discussion, songs, and study of the Communist Revolution and the Great Patriotic War of 1941 to 1945.

At age nine, most young people join the Young Pioneers. Young Pioneers take part in community activities. They spend leisure time in Pioneer palaces, where they might work on hobbies, study sciences, or participate in folk dancing, sewing, or weaving activities.

Top of page: schoolboys stride down a cobbled street in Latvia. A popular after-school organization is the Young Pioneers. Above: a tug-of-war at a Baltic Pioneer camp.

When a child turns fourteen, he or she is ready to join Komsomol, the Young Communist League. Komsomol members have group discussions about history and Communist party activities, and many spend some time on construction projects, on collective farms, and on community service programs.

Most nonfarm Soviet citizens work a forty-hour week. They occupy their leisure time with household chores, getting together for a meal with relatives or friends, watching television, or going to the movies or the theater. Ice skating, ice fishing, and cross-country skiing are favorite winter activities. Millions of Soviet citizens are ice hockey and soccer fans, and there are hockey and soccer leagues for youths and adults in many cities. The circus is also highly popular, and more than six thousand people make their living as circus performers.

Citizens travel within cities and between cities by subway, trolleybus, or train. Cars are relatively expensive—the cheapest costs what the average worker makes in eighteen months, and there is no installment buying. Used cars cost

Field hockey is popular with Soviet fans.

almost as much as new ones, and spare parts can be hard to find. Gasoline is also expensive.

People who can afford it escape to dachas on weekends and for vacations. These country cottages range from single-room shacks to more splendid buildings of several rooms.

National holidays in the Soviet Union include International Women's Day on March 8, Workers' Day on May 1—or May Day—and the anniversary of the Communist Revolution on November 7. May Day and November 7 are occasions for great parades, especially in Red Square in Moscow.

Christmas is not a big holiday, although people do decorate Christmas trees. New Year's Day is the time of gift-giving and the arrival of Father Frost, the Soviet version of Santa Claus.

Nearly every family has a television, and Moscow TV stations reach the entire nation. Each of the fourteen other republics has its own station, and each televises in the republic's main language. Televised sports events, game shows, dramatic shows, movies, and children's puppet shows are the main television fare.

Television programs sometimes feature rock concerts, and rock bands and stars also appear in live concerts. The government tries to control rock music, insisting that it not be exceedingly wild or loud.

Many people living in villages that range from a few hundred to five thousand or more people also enjoy television programs. Many villagers also have refrigerators and other electric appliances. Many villages are cut off from the outside world during the winter and in spring, when roads turn to mud. Rural schools do not have as many resources as those in cities, and, generally, rural people do not attend schools for as many years as city dwellers.

Although the government in the Soviet Union sought to stamp out religion, the Russian Orthodox Church continues to exist there as it has for a thousand years. That church is not nearly as powerful as it once was, however.

The Russian Orthodox Church constitutes the Soviet Union's largest religious group. About fifty million members belong to this faith.

TBS/Reagan

TBS/Reagan

TBS/Reagan

Top of page: *the monumental columns of the Hermitage Museum in Leningrad's Winter Palace.* Above: *part of the museum's collection of icons.*

Other Christian religions include the Armenian Apostolic Church and the Georgian Orthodox Church, along with Mennonite, Pentecostal, Seventh Day Adventist, Baptist, and Jehovah's Witness groups. The Jewish population numbers about two million. Most of the native peoples of Azerbaijan, Uzbekistan, Tadzhistan, Turkmenia, Kirghzia, and Kazakhstan are Muslims. Buddhists can be found in the Buryat Autonomous Republic and the Tuva Autonomous Republic.

Literature, music, and the dance in the world's largest country have long histories, dating far back before the Revolution of 1917. Well-known writers of the period after 1917 have been Maxim Gorky, Valentin Rasputin, and Fyodor Abramov. Outstanding post-Revolution composers have been Aram Khachaturian, Sergei Prokofiev, and Dimitri Shostakovich. The theater remains strong in the Soviet Union, and the more than one hundred children's puppet theaters are immensely popular.

Censorship of artists, especially writers, existed under the czars, and it continued under the Communist government. Throughout

Soviet history, there have been periods of relative freedom for artists as well as periods of severe censorship and even prison for those who criticized communism or the government.

Right: *a performance by Leningrad's Kirov Ballet.* Below: *Soviet composers Sergei Prokofiev (left) and Aram Khachaturian (right).*

TBS/Reagan

SOVFOTO

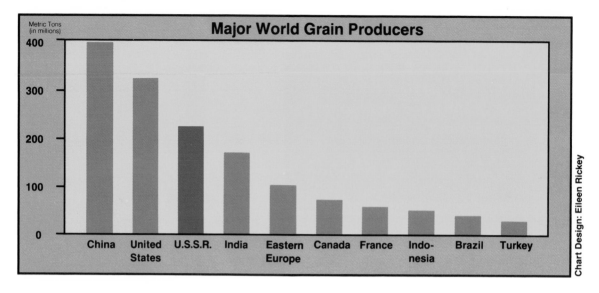

Major World Grain Producers

Metric Tons (in millions)

400 — 300 — 200 — 100 — 0

China | United States | U.S.S.R. | India | Eastern Europe | Canada | France | Indonesia | Brazil | Turkey

ECONOMY, SCIENCE, AND TECHNOLOGY

In the Soviet Union, the government owns land and other natural resources, factories, machines, and all other things needed to produce goods, services, and farm crops. It also owns transportation systems. Government officials decide what and how much will be produced and when and where. The government sets the prices for goods and the wages that farm, factory, and service workers are paid. According to Communist theory, such control over the economy brings the greatest good to the greatest number of people. Under the system, everyone is guaranteed a job and income, and it is illegal for an able-bodied person not to have a job.

The government guides the economy through five-year and one-year plans. Five-year plans set general goals. One-year plans go into much more detail and involve monthly production quotas for factories. Plans pass down from government officials to farm and factory managers who are responsible for carrying them out.

Under five-year and one-year plans, the Soviet Union has produced great amounts of iron and steel, electricity, heavy machinery, oil and natural gas, transportation equipment, and many other goods. However, it often has had trouble meeting goals for food production.

Planning from the top down has had its problems. Planners have long thought in terms of quantity—so many trucks or locomotives, so much iron and steel. Too little attention was paid to quality, and in the effort to meet production goals, managers gave little thought to it either. This especially has been the case with consumer goods, such as household appliances. Many consumer goods also have often been in short supply because of the emphasis on iron and steel and other industrial products. The government long kept the prices of food and some other items below what it cost to produce them, and the government has had to spend billions of rubles a year to make up the difference between cost and price. Controlled prices, along with scarcity, stimulated a black market in the quality goods that were available. Faulty communication and transportation made planning doubly difficult and led to much inefficiency and waste.

Ideas for change in the economy appeared in the 1980s after Mikhail Gorbachev achieved power. There was to be a great emphasis on quality and on the production of consumer goods. Managers and workers would have a greater voice in planning and setting quotas, and workers who did not perform well would suffer cuts in pay. Factories and farms would strive to make a profit, and the prices of goods would be set according to what it cost to produce them. The government would encourage more food production by individual farmers. It would also encourage such skilled workers as carpenters and plumbers to set up businesses for their own private gain.

Reforms have allowed farmworkers to sell the food they produce for their own profit.

TBS/Reagan

Plans for change in the economy called for more use of automated machinery in factories. It was hoped that this would help make production more efficient.

In other areas of science and technology, the Soviet Union had developed the ability to make nuclear weapons by the early 1950s. Then, in 1957, it became the first nation to place an artificial satellite into orbit. In 1961, Yuri Gagarin became the first human to orbit the earth. The Soviet Union moved on to build space stations and to develop plans to send humans to Mars in the 1990s.

In addition, Soviet space probes have circled the moon, landed there, and returned with dust and other specimens. In 1988 the Soviet Union launched its first space shuttle. Unlike American space shuttles, the first one the Soviets placed in orbit had no humans aboard. Computers controlled it.

The Soviet Union's best computer skills and equipment have been used by the military and in the space program. Computers have also been used to some extent in keeping track of five-and one-year plans.

Much of the effort to develop computers in the Soviet Union has been placed on mainframe machines, with little attention to personal computers. Their use had not become widespread by the end of the 1980s, and most personal computers in the nation came from such countries as Japan and the United States.

In the Soviet Union, the government has always guarded information closely. Computers and photocopying machines and other means of storing and exchanging information offer a challenge to that policy.

Like every industrial nation, the Soviet Union has had problems with pollution. The use of coal to produce electric power has added to air pollution. The growing number of automobiles in cities has also added to air pollution. Efforts to reduce the problem have included computerizing traffic control systems to reduce auto stops and starts and planting greenery that thrives on carbon monoxide.

For years factories in the Soviet Union have dumped waste materials into rivers, seriously polluting much of the nation's water. The huge Lake Baikal in central Asia became badly polluted from waste dumping, too. Efforts have begun to reduce water pollution, and Lake Baikal was saved by stopping the dumping of wastes there entirely.

The Aral Sea, also in Central Asia, became another area with severe environmental problems. Drawing water from the lake for irrigation caused much of that sea to dry up. What once was 10,000 square miles (26,000 sq. km) of the lake's water became a salty desert. Restoring the Aral Sea, if that can be done, will be a huge task costing a great deal of money.

Nuclear power plants have been built in the Soviet Union to generate electric power, and there have been accidents. One at Chernobyl, north of Kiev killed thirty people and spread radioactive material over a wide area in 1986. An earthquake in Armenia in December 1988 halted work on some nuclear plants in that area. In spite of accidents and natural disasters, however, the Soviet Union remained committed to a greater use of nuclear power.

Like any industrialized state, the Soviet Union suffers pollution problems. This pulp mill on Siberia's Lake Baikal has been fitted with pollution-control devices.

Galen Rowell/Mountain Light

A Chronology of the Soviet Union

800s The Viking Rurik is the first ruler of Russia. The first Russian state is established. Kiev is the center of government.

988 Vladimir I introduces Christianity to Russia. The Cryllic alphabet is adopted.

1200s Russia comes under Mongol rule.

Late 1400s Czar Ivan III ends Mongol rule.

1547 Ivan IV becomes first crowned czar.

1613 After ten years of civil war Michael Romanov becomes czar. His family will rule Russia for three hundred years.

1703 Peter I founds St. Petersburg; he tries to bring Western ways to Russia.

1812 Napoleon invades Russia with an army of 600,000 but is badly defeated.

1825 Some nobles and army officers demand rule by law. Members of this "Decembrist Revolt" are hanged by Nicholas I.

1861 Alexander II frees the serfs. Some towns gain self-government.

1905 Russo-Japanese war is fought, and Russia is defeated. Nicholas II is forced to establish representative government.

1914-1917 With France and England, Russia enters World War I against Germany and Austria-Hungary.

1917 Revolt forces Nicholas I out. Lenin becomes dictator. The Soviet Union withdraws from World War I.

1918-1921 Civil war with anti-Communists rages.

1922 The Union of Soviet Socialist Republics is established.

1924 Lenin dies, and Joseph Stalin gains power over the Communist party.

1929 Stalin becomes dictator.

1939 World War II begins in Europe.

1941 The Soviet Union enters the war on the side of the allies after being attacked by Germany.

Late 1940s In the years following World War II, the Soviet Union takes over Poland, Hungary, Yugoslavia, and other eastern countries, creating the Iron Curtain.

1953 Joseph Stalin dies and Nikita Khrushchev comes to power.

1956 Khrushchev criticizes Stalin's methods of ruling and announces the philosophy of peaceful coexistence with the West.

1957 The Soviet Union launches *Sputnik I*, the first spaceship to orbit the earth.

1960 The Soviet Union brings down a U.S. intelligence-gathering plane.

1961 Yuri Gagarin becomes the first person to orbit the earth.

1962 Soviet missile bases are discovered in Cuba, causing tension between the United States and the Soviet Union. The bases are later removed.

1964 Khrushchev is forced to retire. Leonid Brezhnev becomes head of the Communist party.

1980-1985 Four heads of government die.

1985 Mikhail Gorbachev becomes head of the Communist party. He announces great changes in the Soviet Union in the form of *glasnost* (openness) and *perestroika* (making over).

1985-1988 Gorbachev and President Ronald Reagan meet five times. The Soviet Union and the United States agree to reduce the number of their nuclear weapons.

1989 The Soviet Union withdraws its troops from Afghanistan and also agrees to cut its armed forces by 500,000.

Map of the Soviet Republics

REPUBLIC	POPULATION*	CAPITAL
Russian S.F.S.R.	144,000,000	Moscow
Ukraine	50,900,000	Kiev
Uzbekistan	18,500,000	Tashkent
Kazakhstan	16,000,000	Alma-Ata
Belorussia	10,000,000	Minsk
Azerbaijan	6,700,000	Baku
Georgia	5,270,000	Tbilisi
Tadzhikistan	4,600,000	Dushanbe
Moldavia	4,100,000	Kishinev
Kirghizia	4,000,000	Frunze
Lithuania	3,600,000	Vilnius
Armenia	3,345,000	Erevan
Turkmenistan	3,200,000	Ashkhadbad
Latvia	2,600,000	Riga
Estonia	1,542,000	Tallin

*Mid-1980s estimate

INDEX

947
Cla

CLARK, JAMES I.

The Soviet Union: A Portrait